COMING TO TERMS WITH GEESE

BY LOIS VAN HOUTEN

Lincoln Springs Press

THE FOLLOWING POEMS HAVE APPEARED OR
WILL APPEAR IN THE FOLLOWING PUBLICATIONS:

STONE COUNTRY: Masks; Olive Tree; Coming to Terms with Geese; Levels
GREENFIELD REVIEW: Wanderers
IMAGES: Believing A White Deer Led Them/The Huns Galloped Westward; Black Dirt; Odyssey; Russian Cemetery; Battles
LIPS: So This Is You/That Person With the Taciturn Mouth/the One With the Beagle Grin; As White Birds; Above the Salt; Living Without Childhood; Gandy Dancers
FOOTWORK: Rose of Sharon; Night Stalker; Falling Through; Missing; Speaking to My Brother
BERGEN POETS: The Gallery; Ice-Tongued; Going to Bed With Animals
SINS OF THE MORNING III & IV: Soundings; From High Point
CENTERING ON THE EARTH ANTHOLOGY: Silences
DUST BEHIND THE DOOR: Boulders
COLORADO NORTH REVIEW: The Slowing Time
JOYING: JOINING OLD & YOUNG: The Revenge of the Woodwife
LUNCH: The Columbarium; Links
SONOMA COUNTY WOMEN'S VOICES: The Sojourner
WOMAN'S NEWSPAPER OF PRINCETON: The Room, Dielieder

Library of Congress Cataloging-in-Publication Data

Van Houten, Lois.
Coming to terms with geese.

Includes index.
I. Title.
PS3572.A4225C6 1986 811'.54 86-27734
ISBN 0-961.7539-0-2

Published by:
LINCOLN SPRINGS PRESS
P.O. Box 269
Franklin Lakes
New Jersey 07417

CONTENTS

PART I

PART II

PART III

PART IV

PART V

PART VI

to Peggy,

Sister Artist,

Endeavorer.

Lois Van Houten

July 27

COMING TO TERMS WITH GEESE

PART I

"When we no longer believe in myths
when they are no longer feasible...
that is the beginning of alienation
the ground-swell of despair."

AS WHITE BIRDS

Four days in this house
they are beginning to come out...
to walk free from the closets
and corners
the stasis memory stacked them in.

Beginning to resume the influence
of brooms and skillets, school books
cluttered on a shelf...
the broken pencils that graffitied
the cellar beams.

Their time slots burgeoning through
filmy veils.

Here is the red vinyl chair
where the man sits, frail yet dominant.
The woman whose false teeth continue
to click after death...
the youth, holding the drum skin
split in a ten year fury.

And they are real enough   as they
pull me in to their thin whisperings;
more so than when they proffered flesh.

Come to us   come to us
they cry. We are the hubris
of your myths...the search
for your lost mercurial selves.

We are your white birds sitting
the cloud's edge
singing snow drops   to the
grass.

THE ROOM

Two years have passed: you've become
a myth to me...
something long and smooth with a tremulous
aura though your daughter has your hands
and the Japanese believe there is no such
thing as by-gones.

In your room where your latest grandchild
lies, I watch the light fall into itself
the shadows burn away in the spinning air.
The stored benevolence of bookish ghosts
unloosed with the darkness
slide back neatly on the shelves.

A ceramic cat grins from a dresser, pleased
with the room's new usage.

Your daughter frowns: she imagines a black
bird signaling at the window; omens and
forebodings.
Her hands clasp the infant to her breast.
This is her first: her myths are not
the same as ours.

OLIVE TREE

My mother lies in her
burnished box in her square
allottment of cemetery earth.
I place a red geranium   feel
at my windpipe the wishbone
of regret.

Call it love/ this friable ambivalence;
call it if you will, the power
of the myth.

Twenty years later, rejection
and desire   swing on the pendulum
of season's change...
the living and the dead   still
fight for recognition on a stony
field.

I wait for the Olive Tree
to tap   take root: a
tough planting for unrewarding
soil.

MASKS

The sun smiles today
ripe and red as a pippin;
it is not always so kind.

Somedays,like us,it frowns
behind the mask.

This then, is the climate
we are born to: this tearing
at tissues
this honed ambivalence.

Building our myths, constructing
masquerades   only to find
in the House of Death there are
no masks:
only the chewed bones
of deception.

We paint hex signs on the window
panes for comfort and luck...
rain comes and sponges them away.
Soon   rain turns acid   and
grows dust.

SO THIS IS YOU. THAT PERSON WITH THE TACITURN MOUTH/THE ONE WITH THE BEAGLE GRIN

Blue ice on garden stone
the morning wide-open as a yawn...
the trees,stoic, in their naked skins.

We walk alone, shouldering our myths:
for loss of one/ a finger dies.

Craving a love no one can give
we live our lives like rows of turnips:
roots tangled, but our fruit contained.

Along the path bushes lean
stripped of foliage and berry.
My black cat weaves/ rubs her pelt
on purple stalks.

Only she knows the subtle strength
of random cries...
her movements pre-determined
like something poured.

ODYSSEY

"Those are your nerves out there
clinging to space.
That is my chin clenched tight
against the burgeoning cold."

A bridge of frost glitters
from a charred sky.
We move/ tugging our shadows   tiny
as ants on the convex sides
of spoons.

The moon disdains our miniscule
obsessions:
the map your fingers print
across my cheek
the incoherent gestures of my passion.

We gather up talismans/ sympathetic
stone
press them against the dark.

(Even our ghosts are heavy-handed
reaching for our throats .)

Cheat us of the ikons of our caring
we are no more than summer lemons
left too long to freeze.

NECESSITY OF MYTHS

We come this way but once
someone said:
windows dripping blood
icicles standing out
of our skulls.

So going into the solstice
into the dark again...the days
cracking walnuts under white
knuckles...
when we break the old myths
across our knees so they dangle
like kindling
that is the beginning of alienation
the ground swell of despair.

Once on the road to Morristown
(a city rich in archeology and myth)
I saw an abandoned house someone had
painted entirely black:
screens, staircases, window frames
and doors...
it stood like a hearse or an unlit
pyre, at the crossroads of being.

Lately, I dream that house: a room
full of butterflies.
They have come in from the cold
and line the walls in all the colors
imagined...
their long bodies pulsing in
tenuous hold.

WE MARRY MYTHS & SO MUST LIVE WITH THEM

dreamers
reluctant to see without
the ingratiating eye.

weary of our blue-veined tongues:

and we crave so   we crave
the feathered days, the daisies
white in their earthern pots.

but slowly   slowly
the core melts down: the
essential fault opens beneath
our feet

and we are lost: poor hands
raised from some devil of a flux
when what we wanted   was the
innocence of flowers.

LINKS

Under the mountains of forever
the mists of time and loss
the barbaric pulse ticks flesh.

A body passes to another   another:
so many links of sausage   parted
on the chopping block.

Stripped down to the basic animal—
a meal, a sheltered place
a mating with a lover
a dance to thwart the vulture's
cackle—

A year bends in a slow curve...
Jupiter and Venus move to a familiar
juxtaposition.
A room, static, waits for the human
rollover/that hitches an ingenious
brain
to the fifth-digited hand.

The full-breasted soil   as always
satisfies the belly of the peddler...
still walking insanely   into
confrontation.

THE CHURCH

For Tess Gallagher

"It is as if the poem acted as a live-in church"

Sometimes we throw out the mind
with the cat
to see what it can scrounge.
The things, the places we have known
cocoons we can crawl into.

Each day, the body marches/a sentry
arms braced against diminishment...
mind, that feisty animal takes loss:
builds it to the temple.

We stare into a hearth's flame:
faces trail smoke from their nostrils.
A woman, beloved, writhes as the fire
guts her skull.

But mind, that sorcerer, binds the spirit
back to flesh
arms pinioned in a velvet jacket
as a falcon to its jesses...
so myth stands mortal/to astonished
recognition.

Only mind can build the church
erect the steeple
open the doors and let in the people.

ANGUISH: THE SINGING OF THE OTHER WORLD

What sort of grief aborts those last
defenses
allows the anguished transport to
the other world...
entering, as the dogwood tree enters
the world of winter:
after the flocks of birds, descending
like the Ninja
after the stripping of its berries.
What kind of pain takes to itself
the white vision of the swan.
There must be the headlong moment
when the old red tomcat, with his last
perilous cry
gives up his earthly station.
Now he is singing to us from the other
world.

PART II

"The flowers of this bush
would burn our flesh."

WORMWOOD

In June the wormwood grows
thick
with the laying on of green:
a woody shrub, yielding a dark
oil
bitter as the taste of gall
the worm curled at the root
coiled in the heart of the summer
people
robbing their bright insouciance.

Summer was a green spoke
in the turning wheel of seasons
when we rendezvoused at the deserted
house.

The day with its pulsing hills
and light
surfaced the wild desires
of our flesh.

Our bodies' thrust denied the checkmate
irony of death:
the wormwood already burgeoning the trees
staining the walls and beams.

The lilacs overblown, faded to a brown
demise.

CHANGELING

This is how it must have been:
this is how the poet assumed
the identity of the changeling.

Here is the dark figure of myself
scheming to catch the brown bird
in the bush
the coral in the belly of a cloud.
Knowing the strange, inciting force
that shaped the lily to an entity.

Here are the artless shadows of our
selves sliding thin   as a
knife slips through
butter.
Crystals of salt/dredged from the earth's
silt.

Here are our proven comrades at the edge
of death:
asking for only a discreet amnesty.

TRAPS

Traps close in around us...
the fear instilled by our fathers
lying, a perfect steel capsule across
our tongues   so reason no longer knows
its name
but shudders   like a rose shredded
on its own thorns...
or stagnates like water caught in hollows
between the thruway and the field.

I saw in an inner-city bar   one
of those caverns dismal as a smoked salmon...
a young girl balanced on a stool:
a pad in her lap   a trap of words
leading the awful hungers of the soul
into a vertigo of grief.

And in the end, embracing those
juggernauts
so many years denied, we welcome them
back:
they were, after all, the things that
made us.

ROSE OF SHARON

The Rose of Sharon leans
on the cabled air...
her bell-shaped petals flushed
as an acolyte's cheek.

Heat coils from the caked soil:
locusts barnstorm the trees
and the afternoon drones on: without
clemency   without reprieve.

I think how a match lit in a closed
garage   how gasoline ignites   a
day explodes.

The flowers of this bush would burn
my flesh.

LILIES

September, sliding into October
one season slouching into another
the pears falling like brass bells
from the trees...
the days passing in a haze of smoke
your face blurred by it, the features
soft as through a scarf of silk.
my fingers unsure of touch   lost
somewhere in the blindness of sight;
the weather no more cut from whole
cloth than overselves...
prone to spawning   these lilies
of despair:
black   in any season.

FROM HIGH POINT

In the beginning, it was
the climb:
a vaporous trail of roses
the nights winking in and out
of the compelling hours
trembling like reeds
in the wind.

Then, the moving out under
a blue warp of sky...
the grasping at myths, blood
channels wide.
The flesh, heated, straddling
the meridian.

Now, it is the commonwealth
of autumn:
the swallows have flown...
a few picked-over rabbits
wait for the vultures.
Underground, old bones weave
in a slow dance.

The maps we followed
to this place
have vanished.

COURTSHIP

All that ivory dawn
jays screeched like cats
hung-up on screens.

Doves unfroze from the creepers.
Sparrows struck sparks
from each other.

In the house, she busied herself
with the usual routine: beds
to be smoothed over
the animals let out, the laundry
sorted.

Outside, everything seemed larger
than itself.
The front-yard maple embraced
the house.
The grandfather pine reached
higher and higher, so that
it became a prince among pines
as the cooing of the doves
was a symbol of love.

"Love," she said, thinking
of her lastest episode...
How she'd been carried beyond her wildest
imaginings
on fiery wings.

She wished for a small, brown bird
to woo her.

THE SLOWING TIME

The red rooster waggles his comb
and scratches at fallen leaves.
The sun slices through yellow...
There is all that filtered light
as the color-wheel winds down.
It is right to withdraw
from the green passion of summer.
But the fire still prevails though
we step back   hold it aside:
like that caught match in your hand
that waits for a certain striking.
How strange   this keeping
of the flame...
even these trees you stroke
with your fingers;
marching doggedly through the brambles
with their slowed sap inside.

CAROUSELS

A finch is singing from a maple
branch: "Needle and thread
                        Needle and thread"
it stitches my heart.
A thrush joins in spilling silver
thimbles.

How we long for such purity
thrashing against the fisher's
net.

The old devils cry their dark
dichotomy
the words of the poets,
an insupportable humming,
craze in our ears.

We are all of us schizophrenics
in a field of babel
white ducks skimming the lake
yellow beaks caught in soda-can
tabs.

Even the clock is awry in its striking
as it wakes mornings sewn into time.

VIOLETS

That spring
the violets were everywhere
casting blue shadows
on late snow.

Naked
we came   and there was no night.
Only the sun, full and bursting
as a pomegranate.
Only our fleshed incandescence.

How quickly we smothered it
under the hour's glass;
how quickly   our glow-worm
for the dark.

There is much to be said   for the
existential stance:
the smell of honeysuckle furring
the nostrils...
the incredible pyro-technics
of holiday rockets.

That first kiss stacking the cards
in the memory box.

The preference for violets.

BLOOD OF ROSES

Imagine a room sealed off by snow
but snow inside, too...falling
in slow peaks on the tops of potpourri
and pills;
settling in a blue vase.
Imagine icicles growing in this room
like stalactites   hugging the ceiling
and the walls
frozen in a static dance.

Imagine your mind, wintry and webbed
over.
How it would go into that crystal
world like a white shadow.
How it would dream of shadows spliced
under river ice;
espaliered, like those Japanese dwarf
trees   up chilled walls.

Imagine trying to breathe in such a place:
the breath coming back to you   heavy
with frost.
How your body might stiffen in a frozen
gesture...
but how   you might also   at some
moment, thinking of others   receive
that kiss of life, which is warmer
than the blood of roses on the snow.

PART III

"For part of us forever lives
with animals."

SILENCES

Don't let the bear
be routed from its woods
or your ragged shadows
slay the deer.

Know they are creatures of the land:
their blood ebbs and flows as yours
your seasons clock as theirs.

Know that the land is with you
always
throbbing its great pulse
under your cliffs of glass.

But what strange unrest nags
like a beggar, behind your eyes
and sends you upcountry at sunset
to the fields and hills, folding
themselves to silence...
the clouds massing to mauve and gold.

Know, as you breathe in the air's
continuance   you are the
stranger.

LEVELS

The apples are falling
without a sound...
the quail, shot from the hunter's
sky
quivers and dies.
We hold tight/uncertain grace
to thwart despair.

We feed the bear
that monolith on noiseless feet
who comes to our charity
from nightwood.
His great head bows
his small and dangerous eyes
meet ours;
between us/recognition fleshes out
the knife.

The leaves like wingless birds
sail past:
we drift as narrow sleepers, our
bloods' thin hands.
We fear the hunters bold
among ouselves...
Riding their long black guns.

NIGHT STALKER

It is this way with me:
I sleep with my toes clenched
inward, dreaming of a willow
branch that crosses over.
It is not where the willow leans
to   but that it reaches out...
that it shoots tendrils
to the blue shelf of summer night.
That it yearns for the bird:
for the tight clutch of spiraled claws
the body/tensing song.

It isn't every bird sings at night
or is a night stalker   or a
threader of thunder...

Or soars past diners at the twentieth
floor level: its wide mouth a scoop
to suck in gnats and dreamers.

COMING TO TERMS WITH GEESE

This goose balanced
on one foot
this perfect equilibrist;
this day's merry-go-round
of sun stripes and water fowl.

This moment   breakable
curiously   refractive:
light poised like plexiglass
over a fish bowl.

These geese, paddling a world
on edge;
ourselves, clutching a clump
of daffodils...

Trying to solace
make peace with our bleak
and dangerous hearts...

As we ride the carousels
ring the bells:
leaving a trail of tiny bones
a trace of featherless
bodies.

GOING TO BED WITH ANIMALS

I sleep in my thicket of bones
my animal curled inside.

Small cat purrs
            in the curve of my back.
We rock in the Kingdom of Beasts
where all bed down together
            or wake to fury of teeth and claw.

All day in my body bag
inside its truss of flesh
I speak to the growling one:
            "Sit" "Lie down" Be human if you can.

Then night with its heavy mouth
intones: Be free, now, dream
            of petaled things or bloodied...

But cling always to the other one:
savor its warmth, its love...
            its company.

For part of you forever moves
(in the deep forest of your brain)
            with animals.

SOUNDINGS

As the woman lay dying, they said,
a small brown bird broke
from the palm of her hand
beating its wings frantically
around the room, until, through an open
window it flew to the wide soundings
of the sky.

Later, near the lake after a day's quick
thaw,
you heard something knocking under the ice.
"It's the old man who lives there," they
told you.
Thud, thud   his heavy fists bang
on his glass overcoat.
A crack opens one sleeve.
The collar bulges.
You needed to see him burst straight-up
shattering the ice to needle-points
of spray
but it was only the lake   measuring its
strength   taking soundings.

ICE-TONGUED

for Theresa who saw the vision

It was that day in the woods
the trees turned crystal
ice-tongued to bells
grew from the ground
in prisms.

It was that day
the dogs baying ahead
into the sun   printing their paws
on the crusted snow

We saw the bird
frozen to the branch
all ice and gleaming:
a scarlet bell   its
tongue cased in glass.

BELIEVING A WHITE DEER LED THEM/ THE HUNS GALLOPED WESTWARD

white deer
nuzzling a crystal pool
crossing a blue leap
of winter sky
to trail/like a white sash
numbed stalks of trees.

white spirit
under a snow moon's halo
hallowed in old legends:

misty tales of Huns
galloping snowy steppes...
westward/the albino one
drifts like swamp gas
under a shrouded moon.

under the sun/bleached white
like coral...the horses thundering

avid   as love rising:
but love must cool/its shadows
darken and fade.

the white deer leaves no shadow
but a white glow/blazed
across a world.

REVENGE OF THE WOODWIFE

The house was strange: it suffered
a malaise of the spirit. It smelled
of dead birds.
Green-eyed cats lay in positions of watch
waiting for subterranean signals to begin.

Doors, windows opened wide and hung loose.

The woman returned, taking up her position
on the humped-back couch.
Pouring herself a glass of red, she stared
through the crystal at a deep forest where
rabbits were tall with long bony ears.

When her husband arrived, scoffing
at her fancies
she would warn him for the last time.

From the spare bedroom, where the animals
ate
came the sound of scuffling: the animals
were back   it was her delight   this bringing
the forest into the dwelling.

Let him come, laughing his short, harsh bark.
He would be told of the danger: of the bandit
raccoons who would enter the kitchen   to
cart him away—kicking.

PART IV

"We are the quin-tes-cen-tial childhood guardian of the human mythos."

WANDERERS

I.
Emma Alone

What is she looking for: Emma
alone on the street at six a.m.
her long, white nightgown under a yellowed
robe;
pale skin, winter hair   ghosting
the neighborhood.

Is she looking for Joe?
Joe was killed in World War II.
Ethel died of a hemorrhage. Lolly she lives
with. Lolly is mean. But maybe that's not
Lolly at all but Sarah.

How lovely is the morning: a golden-haired
day
as she was once a blue-eyed blonde
with Prince the shepherd by her side.
She talks to herself and hears him bark:
but nothing's clear.

Are these her thoughts   or have those watchers
on the porch/pulled them from some other's heart
and mouth.

Now we obscure with question-marks, her solitary
search.
She can't remember seeing us before.

II
Prince

The overlarge shepherd dog ambles alone
in a particularly aimless fashion.
His brindled fur is patchy and dry; he
wears no collar   no I.D. tag.
He sniffs the ground but the scent's been
misplaced in the dripping caves
of his nostrils.

Emma turns the corner. Her robe has come
loose and is dragging.
She is muttering to herself, gumming
the words.

Her eyes regard the sidewalk   the batteries
behind them fluttering weakly.
The shepherd spots her, raises his snout.

She blinks: can this be Prince, the loved
and lost.
He comes alert...barks warily...they seem
to drift into each other.
She stretches out her hand   strokes solid
air.

Was he really there, or was it the dog next
door?
We watch her   she trips and falls   we pick
her up and start her off again like a poorly
wound clock.

III
Joe

Now here's Joe: 34th Infantry in the Pacific
Company C   search and destroy.
Twenty years old: he's walking toward her
with a hole in his head.

"Joe   Joe" she wants to reach out to him
take him to herself but the wound's so terrible.

She blinks, wipes her eyes...and here he is all
fine again, dressed in his civies with his hair
long and curly at the ends.

He was/he is her son. But no. How can he be
anyone at all when he is not.
"Joe, Joe   come home...your father's waiting."
Don't let them catch you as they caught me.
She wishes she were gone herself, or does she?

Now we, the watchers have watched enough.
We come down from the porch, take her by the arms.
It is time for her to go back: though not quite
yet to sleep.

FALLING THROUGH

Clouds the color of a dove's grey wing:
the inbetweenness of winter and autumn.

By nightfall, the sky has come closer
the fog settled over the road
like a second skin.

Long-fingered wraiths slip cauls
over the headlamps
and faces, fallen through the weave
of days rise to be close again.

We slide forward: a nightmare to drown in.
Primordial, the old bones float up
from the bottom
dragging their myths.

THE TRAIN

"Dreams they tell us
can mean many things:
sacred toy-boxes
gilded grottoes."

I dream of traveling: a seat
on a moving train.
In the place next to me   the man
who is closest to my life.
The cars are crammed with pale
passengers
silent as tethered balloons.
Outside, crows rise just in time
as they snatch a bit of carrion
from the track.
I wait to dismount   a certain station
the engineer knows: not I.
We stop at a dreary platform   I nudge
my companion (he does not heed) jump
off to a heavy downpour.
I call his name: the passengers roused
from their lethargy   jeer.
He hears them   now he rises   he's
at the door/foot poised on the iron step
but the engine has begun to pull
and picks up speed.
He shrugs his shoulders   disappears.
In the last car, someone has cleared
a circle in the sooty window and is peering
out.
It is my mother. She has been dead   now
more than twenty years.

LIVING WITHOUT CHILDHOOD

I see it through sheets of rain
crazed waterfalls...
ahead by the side of the road
always.
A squat, grey square of a building:
a broad over-hang of roof, as if
to thwart my spying.

*"This dream from which I do not
wake."*

Louisa is at the black-board her
chalk dancing like a finger on a broom.
Julian is picking his nose...
Renee, wrinkling her brow under its bright
spring of curls.
Paul is caught in rapt connivance
with a paper clip.
The teacher recites: her voice seems
to come from the hollows of her bones.

*"This is a dream from which we never
fully awake."*

She is always sending this message: I
receive it over and over.

The room broods having its own goals:
the pupils immobile as stacks of books.
The teacher reads on...raising her eyes
as if to prick my distant dreaming:

*"We are the quin-tes-cen-tial childhood
guardian of the human mythos.
Lose us and you lose the world."*

GRANADOS PLAYS GRANADOS

Enrique Granados, drowned
with the Sussex in a German torpedo sinking
lives again and plays his Spanish
melodicos across this bleak New Jersey
day.

Listening to the music
the brilliant Arabesques
the singing melodic line...
I reach out from the cell of myself:
"Quasi Ad Libitum."

All morning I've had this feeling
of displacement, even of transport.

Snow swirls outside the window
whirls like gnats around a Japanese
lantern...
settles in the spare linears
of the old school—and I am back, that
teacher, young in years.
Dance time and the children
parade in their little ghost
gowns, their small bodies bending
to this place of warmth—

What is it we want from each other
anyway?
except *por companero* the partner
at the ball.

The music, recorded to discs from old
player-piano rolls   plays on:
ineluctable as sorrow
remote as plums fallen from summer trees.

The drowned man's hands reach
from the waters of the icy Atlantic
to hold this day.

THE GALLERY

She had always known
it would come to this:

The walk down the marble hall
the diorama of her youth   middle
now later years   hung in mid-air
so many slices from a fruit...
a green light playing over them
like sometimes seen before a storm.

Here, a three-cornered hat
the child, awkward   tinder
for the flame.

A miasma of linking years:
the strata shifted...
the schist brittle and dulled.

So many artifacts, animals, rooms;
a soiled doily holding her birthday.

Even old chamber-pots and phonograph
cylinders:
canaries standing in their lemon cages.

And all the while   the way into
and the way back out...
a fine jumble of color and line.

SURFACINGS

The way reflections slide
along a brookside tree
the light, rippling like water
or like blood...
rising from channels/not to flood
but   to touch   with a kind
of love.

(to know more than we do)

The dappling in and out of space:
as an Irish peasant girl catches
blue sky
between the rain drops in her eyes.
Chases hunger
(that mongrel in the chicken yard)
with a single potato:
its white eyes already planted
in the soil.

How later, in another time and place
her daughter's daughter
presses a red leaf to her cheek
glad for its bright stain/against
the dark and stifling pines.

Glad of her bloods surfacing...
unlike this bloody autumn: its
stark red tide   its atavistic
tongue.

AT THE RUSSIAN CEMETERY

Walking through the Russian burial grounds
the names on the tombstones
some in geometric Slavic script
stare at me:
Ivanovitch, Gorka, Polozoff, Wanca.

One time White Russian Imperialist officers
their gold-braided uniforms unraveled
over bones.
Peasants from the bottomless, black dirt
of the Ukraine
the earth, even now, creeping from their
fingernails.

They are all lying down   together in this
place:
escaped from their heritage into the common
end.

Colonel O, of the Imperial Chevalier Guards
unhorsed with his Czar.
Princess M, lamenting her dacha near Toule,
the buffets after the Borzoi hunts.
Sasha the Tarter, who loved his Russian earth,
transplanted to another.

Staring back at a pink marble urn
now stippled with the dust of an afternoon
shower
I see through the mist to another Easter:
my mother in a hat of velvet and roses
dyed on my memory like those painted
pysanky
that woke the Ukraine from a winter
of sleep.

Holding to this talisman, I wake you
mother
as I mark the lilies on the graves
of strangers.

BOULDERS

I remember, thirty years ago
the house with the brick front:
"Don't buy it," my father said...
"there'll be water in the cellar;
go farther up the hill."

Did I ever think of his advice
as I passed every day.
Thirty years   thirty years
up and down   up and down
scrambling from low to high
our flesh moving in boots
of sod.

My father knew what he was talking
about
watching us push our boulders
of pain.

BLACK DIRT

The land under the hawk's wing
flattens, unrolls to a low horizon;
imprints in its cynic's eye   a
deep, endless black.
The bird, from far above, hones in
on small fur; dives and snatches
with surgical precision.

Shuback steps out of his back door
sees the HAWK OF THE MARSH; his fingers
itch for the stock of his gun   but
the onions are waiting   the harvesters
gathered: the men brown as seasoned
chestnuts
the women unshapely in head rags
and layers of clothing.

The bird floats lazily. The onion pickers
clump to the fields; black dirt clinging
to their heels.
They sing out their names: Shuback, Jaroz
Trezenski, Tomazewski...
stare from eyes a bright, washed blue.

When a son of Shuback marries
the priest instructs: "Take this woman
she will dress you in black.
Take this land   this black dirt
this gold."

ORCHIDS

"...orchids," you said, studying
their pictures...you admired their
high color.

In the old movies
you are hiding your life behind
your hands, as though they were
orchids.

At the zoo, refraining from the pleasures
of your family
you turn aside as they feed with their
long white fingers, the zebra, the hippo
the giraffe

and by the seal pen, all you can think of
are thick, masculine stems
showy blue-red petals, as the others
laugh and laugh at the wet and slippery
mammals standing on their tails.

You never smiled: even when your son
younger then
climbed the tree house in the park
his eyes opaque with their brown pupils
serious, wondering if he pleased.

Was it the lack of elegance and polish:
the mother, vulgar and spewing venom.
The brother soon dead from alcohol
and drugs...
the husband, violent when he drank?

Was it the lives of women wanting
something more?

Orchids were your style: alien and remote
cool in all that torrid heat.

Others made do with daffodils or tulips.

GANDY DANCERS

Remember those advent calendars?
How each day, another set of shutters
or a small paper door/ opened
to the unexpected.
Could this be her life?
Excitement revving to a high pitch;
doors and windows flying wide
to her prying fingers.
A life like a kaleidoscope: full
of color and light...too fleeting
to be troublesome.
Nothing too little or too much...
the dance card always filled. No
friends stealing hearts from mouths
or gandy dancers, pretending to be real.
Her life would be a college balloon
floating over sex and bare-legged
booze.
"F" she said to those who tried
to bring her down.
"F" "F you"...when they tried to pick
her up and set her straight.

And so it was: "F" to all even
to the end.

PART V

"There are things that are edible
and things that can kill...
you have to walk between them."

DIE LIEDER

Lieder, drifting from the gramophone
the bel-canto of the baritone   smooth
as the bowl of Uncle's pipe.

We children gather in the playroom
awed by the Sunday ritual: the smell
of tobacco, the Weltschmerz of the music...
the library, with its leather-topped tables
where the wood-fire leaps to its own conclusion;
my Uncle Charley, their German born father
Charles...strokes his white meerschaum
listens gravely to a mellower century.

My cousins and I play Parcheesi, Dominoes
all we are allowed, Sabbath.
Uncle snaps his fingers military fashion
at a winning yell.

How tender it seems, how long ago:
before space   before the bomb...
Before the passing of fifty years   like pebbles
thrown against the window glass.

Today, I read in the Sunday Review   how
through memory of the past   we become
our present...how we draw strength from memory
for an uncertain future.

"Not so", I mutter.
Where is the strength in a century of anguish?
Die Lieder lost in random fall.

HOLINESS OF OLIVES

Mt. Olive, the highway sign flashes
and my mind somersaults to the small
white church
the country Sunday School
I was sent to summers.
And there I sit on a small, runged chair
next to Honey Barr of the curved, golden hair...
while in the room next to us, her sisters
Edrith and Ruthie
shake their paper-coiled curls, fat as sausages
topped with out-sized bows of pink and yellow.
My own hair, unsplendidly Buster Brown
skims the bertha of a tangerine dress
sewn by my mother.

I wait, fidgety and bored, until the passing-out
of cards.
The cards are wonderful: shiny and pictured
with Bible verses on one side,
men and women in flowing robes of bright colors
and sometimes the man with the yellow circle
around his head, wearing a pure, white dress...
on the other.

But the one card I find in my hand that I
really like
shows a large green mountain with dark trees
on one side of it
and printed on the bottom, MT. OF OLIVES...
and so quiet and so cool looking in that
stuffy classroom...I want to get there
and wonder; what am I doing in this country
church
with these dry-as-dust Barrs
when I could be tasting
the HOLINESS OF OLIVES.

ABOVE THE SALT

I think of salt
its simple chemistry
its spry utility...
its preservation of hams.

How it entered our language
with tenacious hold: "He must
earn his salt," my father said.

How someone's wife with the evil
eye threw over her shoulder
a thimble of salt.
And someone's brother became unlucky
when he spilled the stuff
in his sister's lap.

Now I rock in my bed this winter night
as I rocked in the salt of my mother's
womb.
My animals lie curled head to toe:
it is twenty below.

I recall a custom from the ancestral
salt:
how a great and gleaming silver cellar
was placed in the middle of a long table.
How the favored ones were ranked
at its head.
How they sprinkled with zest
with little thought of flesh or bone
or the falling snow.

THE COLUMBARIUM

The sanctuary for urns stands
on a knoll at the park of the dead.
Its shaft of granite and limestone
glints in the sun...
rises in all weathers, over a hundred
feet.
It is a columbarium from the Latin
meaning dovecote: a place of peace
and love.
Inside its heavy metal doors, marble
walls are recessed and honey-combed
with urns.
There is utter silence.

Somewhere at the top of the tower
a carillon begins to ring in slow
reverberations.
We stare at a bronze staircase set
with emblems of the Zodiac...
Think how time passes
how there is no stopping it.
How it is a given, like gravity
or death.

The room is solemn, austere.
We return to the park where a chill
wind of March skims over markers.
Remember how it is written,
in the local chronicles, that Indians
once dwelt here.
Lenni-Lenape constructed their wigwams
and left their bones   deep
in the soil.

Later, Colonial troops at war
with the British
made this their campground...
cleaned their weapons and readied
their gear
for the battles of the living.

GHOSTS

On the film of dawn
the negatives show their small
ghost-bodies
thin wafers floating the mist.
The light quickens: the sun hauls
itself up like a pumpkin.
An oriole burns orange into the emulsion
and wings whir from sudden green.

I have snapped a kingbird here
mornings, on a dead tree
alert as a policeman waiting the arrest.

Today, early as it is
an old man sits his mower on his strip
of land.
I take him with the lens of my eye;
imagine in the width of his back
the firm lines of the boy...
how his hair must have sprung
from the base of his skull.

I know how it is with him, as in friends
once known
the ghost image of boy or girl
in that first strong fix.

On the stream, a female mallard herds her
flock to shore.
Two males bear her down, head forced
into muddy waters.
She, frantic, struggles free
from their spread and rolls away
fearful for her chicks.

Fearful of the ghosts in the pictures
of her genes.

FAMILY PRIDE

It lies undisturbed
under the sun's paw
and the drift of rain
wedged between the abandoned
greenhouses
and a sputter of family cottages.

Forsythia has scribbled in the boundaries
with a yellow crayon.

The old man is over here; rootstock
of this burgeoning clan, he carries
the name of an early Dutch settler.
He rests with his spouse, flanked
by their sons: Edward, Henry, Jacob
and John.

The headstones lean full-tilt or
have fallen so they lay like the strewn
contents of a cracker-box: their carved
inscriptions rubbed thin by weather
their birth and death dates rousing
no bells.

There is no one who knows anymore
the origin of this place: was it
a corner of a farm set aside
for the convenience of the dead
or a symbol of family pride.

No matter...someone living must care
for it, for the grass is clipped short
as a recruit's hair.

There is a paper carnation or two
faded a pale pink
and even now, a live one leans redly
in a tin can labeled: Campbell's
Tomato Soup.

THE DINER

They decided to go to the diner.
The residue of the day's heat
hung like a charred cloud.
They carried it with them into the dining
room.
She ordered her usual ham with pineapple
sauce and nibbled at it
unable to get her mind off the stone
she carried in her groin.
She told herself there were worse stones,
real or imagined, to carry.

It was necessary to eat, though it seemed
a charade, the people at their tables
unwilling performers.
A woman in a red dress played out a fantasy
with shrimp.
A man attacked his steak with great hostility.
A voice from her childhood seemed to speak:
"Eat slowly, chew well," but there was only
the grey-haired waitress slumped in her traces
as she served the meal.

Her life was taking off to such a degree
there was barely room for her in it.
She must forget about the stone.
She must forget how much she cares for her
body; how desperate she is.
She shifted uncomfortably in the straight-
backed chair.
The stone was pressing like a burning star.
If it kept on, it would burn through.

BATTLES

The cicada are playing their doom song
again...
the birds, restless, lurk in the highest
leaves.
Heat gathers in the afternoon sun
slowing the body's rhythm
so it hangs...heavy as a bog.
It is August: month of loss and disappearance.

The boy was ready: always in August he took
his battles to the last acreage of the woods
to live on berries and what he could catch
in the stream.

He brooded, "As how he'd be missed,"
as he practiced throwing the rope over the branch
a slip knot tied in a lower loop.
He'd read in the papers about a boy
who had done it
and imagined his head gone slack to one side
his eyes bulging, jeans caught at the weight
of his hips.

It is hard for a boy to become a man
to brush the spiders from his eyes and offer
himself to the light.

The silence wrapped him in a warm blanket
fed him like the berries and the stream.
He remembered the conservationist's lecture:
"There are things that are edible
and things that can kill...
you have to walk between them."

MEN & BOYS

I know how boys get
to be armies of men.

A boy finds a stone on the ground
fetches it, fondles it for heft...
raises it past his ear, swings
back his arm and lets go.

The farther it travels
the taller he grows.
Wherever it lands, it burns
into tomorrow.

I once knew a boy who never sighted
when he threw.
His arm had an instinct for apples
a pane of glass, the window of a car
an old woman's favorite rose bush
where petals sheared off like rain.

"Control," they told him, "is the secret.
You must aim straight, then wing it
into the target
for the perfect kill."

MISSING

This is where she disappeared
from this house, set in a triangle
of black.

How heavy the sky
dark the woods.
How uncompromising
the small creatures of the land.

The mountains crouch like rabid dogs.
The lake whispers empty secrets
to the shore.

Days stumble by, muttering to themselves.
Is she up there, held in the steel claws
of the cold
or in some room in the city
where eyelids bleed behind the curtains.

Each night takes over with its horror show
of rancor and regret.
How could her childhood have been so mixed
with bitter aloes?

A week passes...a month.
The moon leans
Somewhere a night bird laughs into dawn.

If she comes back
what will you say...
WHAT WILL YOU SAY?

BIG TEN

I watched him at the party
as he bent down for another can of beer
a young man in his thirties, bearded
and blond...
and listened as he spoke to the young
woman in the cranberry-red shorts and bra:
"The thing is, we never fought."
"Then what was it?" "Why did you get
divorced?" she asked.
"I don't really know,"he replied.
"Maybe because she couldn't get pregnant
or because her job paid better than mine
or maybe it was her mother's interfering."

I thought of my grandmother and the grand-
father I never knew
and how did she stand it when he came home
drunk pay-days with the money spent
and wouldn't have gotten that far if the horse
weren't harnessed to his milk wagon.
How did grandmother ever know that black
was black but also several shades of gray
and the same for white...
And what adds up to 0 one year
may be a big fat ten, another.

SPEAKING TO MY BROTHER

Brother , I am here
sitting at the marker
where you lie.
What can one say to one long dead?

I have heard the prayers of the left
behind
rise like a drone of locusts
as though there were an audience
for supplication.

Today, in the tall building this park
has raised for the living   I saw
a man, work-worn, who it seemed would
have been more at home behind a hammer
or a wheel...
sit for as long as it took to grumble
his chagrin and pain...
rapping his fingers on the marble bench
as though at his kitchen table.

Brother
How can we make sense of what we do
not know:
                    I live   you lived
                    I am   you were
I would like to offer you once more
a can of your favorite beer.

ARCHETYPES, MINIATURES & SIMILARITIES

The cupola on the roof of the red
brick
its design a copy of a colonial
archetype
is eight-sided, painted white
with its own roof of gilded metal.
On its dome stands a weather-vane
pointing north to south...
and over the arrow
an eagle mounted on a gold ball.
The wooden frame of the cupola
is louvered...
a sparrow has built a nest there
unintimidated by the impressive figure
of the bird above.

Three gulls fly over a wing-tip
like military police
followed by five ducks, swimming through
air like barges.

Yesterday in a field outside of town
hobbyists flew their gasoline-powered
model planes;
one a perfectly tooled miniature
of a Beechcraft Staggerwing.

Painters in the eighteenth century
portrayed children of the upper classes
dressed as small adults: the girls
in fine lace gowns, ribbons,with perhaps
a tiny pair of red slippers peeking out
from beneath.
The boys with heavily brocaded waist-
coats, breeches of satin set off
by white stockings and shoes with large
silver buckles.

One portrait by John Durand, shows
"Two Little Boys In A Garden..."
Oddly enough, their over-large heads
topped by fashionable periwigs
could be those of adult subjects.
The poses, almost always formal,
the children gazed from eyes cool
candid and a trifle calculating.

PART VI
for Alice

" I must empty out my mind for this acceptance... this new, Immaculate Death."

PETALS

The cat hauls her black-furred
hide
across the softly-crusted snow.
Falling again, it pales on her coat

like your face from the hospital bed:
pale as white petals against the
institutional sheets.

I think of your patience, your strength.
Your belief in death as pure white promise.

The cat shakes loose   lifts a paw...
moves to the edge of the yard and stops.
She stares with that total stillness
of all stopped things

when the quarrels and cries of a brutal
day
are drawn into the utterances of silence.

Listening, she hears something beyond
perhaps:
something further.

AGAPE

When she steps through that door
to nowhere
the flesh flying from her bones
the skin unpeeling...
When the bones lose their hold
and fall apart...
we will take them
fit them neatly into their plan
flesh out the hollows   stretch skin
and smooth it firmly in place.
We will hang a bodice, a smock, put
arch into sock
and resurrect her in the extravagence
of creation.

THE SOJOURNER

You are held in crystal:
snow stipples your breasts
weeps from your hair...
folds the edges of your world
where we would like to keep you
resting on the invisible.
But the crystal shatters...
a door opens on a high plateau
and there is all that brilliant
light.
The path you came by / whips loose
twisting and turning like an angry
wire.
You look back, wave your hand:
your eyes are terrible   having
shown us the way.

ANNUNCIATION

If I could tell you the loathing
the fear
that this thing brings me...

How I wait at night for the dawn
to tell me differently...
(but the sun rises, as usual,
indifferent.)

How I sense the lilies cold on
their stems
taking the light into themselves
to feed their hunger...

And hear my prayers glance off
solid rock
to thin in air.

I must empty out my mind for
this acceptance: this new
Immaculate Death.

Lois Van Houten was awarded a New Jersey State Council On the Arts Fellowship for 1981 and 1985. She also has received grants from The Geraldine R. Dodge Foundation, Poets & Writers of New York, Inc.; and City of Lyndhurst Cultural Council.

Her five previously published books of poetry are: North Jersey Blues (Cycle Press, 1972); Behind the Door (Stone Country Press, 1976); The Woman Who Warped With Doors (Stone Country Press, 1977); The Woman Wedged In the Window (Vega Press, 1979); and All Those Bells (Stone Country Press, 1981).

She has read at Drew University, Fairleigh Dickinson University, Montclair State College, Ramapo College, William Paterson College, Bloomfield College, Bergen Community College, Passaic County Community College, Morris County College and many poetry centers and libraries throughout the United States.

Her poems have appeared in Greenfield Review, Colorado North Review, Off Our Backs, Dark Horse, Wind Magazine, Epos, Lips, Journal of New Jersey Poets, Footwork, Advance Token to Boardwalk... Anthology of Poets & Writers of New Jersey, and many others.

She is a member of Poets & Writers of New York, Inc., Ramapo Collective, and Bergen Poets.